THE UNITED STATES GOVERNMENT

STATE GOVERNORS

FRANCIE DOLAN

NorwoodHouse Press

Cataloging-in-Publication Data

Names: Dolan, Francie.
Title: State governors / Francie Dolan.
Description: Buffalo, NY : Norwood House Press, 2027. | Series: The United States government | Includes glossary and index.
Identifiers: ISBN 9781978581586 (pbk.) | ISBN 9781978581593 (library bound) | ISBN 9781978581609 (ebook)
Subjects: LCSH: Governors--United States--Juvenile literature. | State governments--United States--Juvenile literature.
Classification: LCC JK2447.D65 2027 | DDC 352.2321302373--dc23

Published in 2027 by
Norwood House Press
2544 Clinton Street
Buffalo, NY 14224

Designer: Rhea Magaro
Editor: Tricia Hoffman

Photo credits: Cover, p. 1 Maxx-Studio/Shutterstock.com; cover, p. 1 Sergey Kamshylin/Shutterstock.com; p. 5 Vector Mine/Shutterstock.com; p. 7 Senior Airman Katelynn Jackson; p. 8 Bob LoCicero/Shutterstock.com; p. 9 Joshua Qualls/Shutterstock.com; p. 10 Thomas Trompeter/Shutterstock.com; p. 11 Paul Brady Photography/Shutterstock.com; p. 12 University of College/Shutterstock.com; p. 13 State of Texas; p. 14 National Guard Bureau; p. 15 Frame Stock Footage/Shutterstock.com; pp. 16-19 Wikipedia; p. 17 Max Goldberg/Iowa State Daily; p. 21 lev radin/Shutterstock.com;

Printed in the United States of America

CPSIA compliance information: Batch #CSNHP27: For further information contact Norwood House Press at 1-800-237-9932.

TABLE OF CONTENTS

STATE GOVERNMENTS

The United States is a union of 50 states. Each state has its own government. State governments make and **enforce** state laws.

Just like the **federal** government, each state government has an **executive** branch, **legislative** branch, and judicial branch. The governor of each state is part of the state's executive branch.

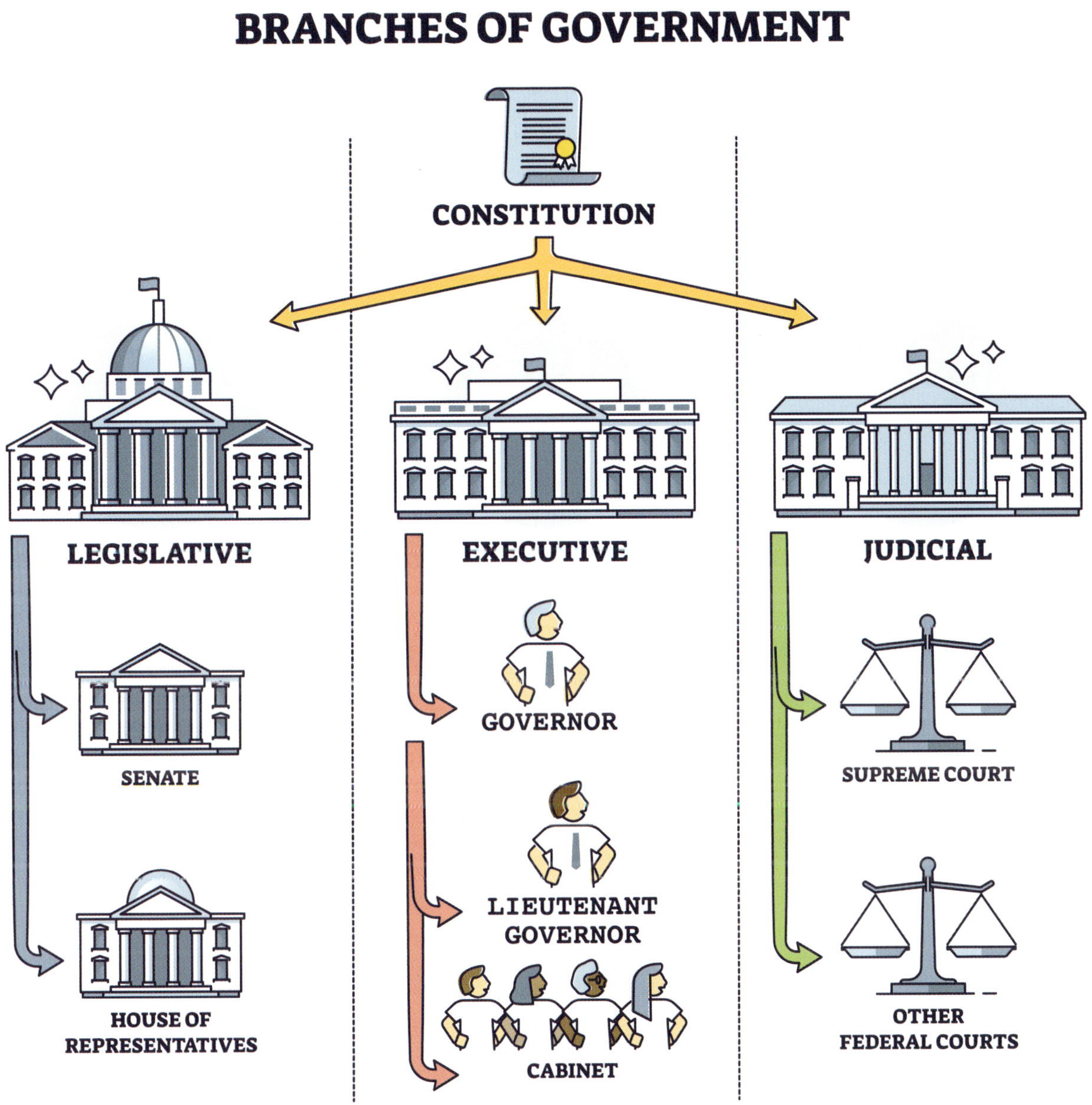
BRANCHES OF GOVERNMENT
CONSTITUTION
LEGISLATIVE
EXECUTIVE
JUDICIAL
SENATE
GOVERNOR
SUPREME COURT
LIEUTENANT GOVERNOR
HOUSE OF REPRESENTATIVES
CABINET
OTHER FEDERAL COURTS

STATE C.E.O. (CHIEF EXECUTIVE OFFICER)

The governor leads the state government. He or she signs or **vetoes** laws passed by the state legislature. Once laws are passed, it is the governor's job to carry them out and make sure they are obeyed.

GREAT SEAL OF THE STATE OF ARIZONA

Voters in each state elect their governor. In 48 states, the governor is elected for a **term** of four years. In Vermont and New Hampshire, the governor is elected for only two years.

Many states limit governors to two terms.

Some states have no term limits.

Many states require the governor to be at least 30 years old. In most states, governors must be U.S. citizens. They must live in the state they govern.

In 45 states, the governor lives in a large house called the Governor's Mansion. Alabama, Michigan, and New Jersey also have beach houses for their governors.

Governors **appoint** people to lead parts of the state government. These may include the Department of Health or the Department of Motor Vehicles.

Governors help manage the state's money. Each year, they submit a **budget** to the state legislature for approval. They give a State of the State speech to tell people how the state is doing.

The governor commands the **National Guard**. He or she orders troops to help during emergencies and natural disasters.

The governor can make executive orders. These are special rules that do not require approval by the state legislature. The governor also has the power to **pardon** criminals.

UNITED STATES GOVERNORS

Before he was elected president, Thomas Jefferson served as the governor of Virginia.

Terry Branstad was the governor of Iowa for 22 years.

The actor and bodybuilder Arnold Schwarzenegger was the governor of California from 2003 to 2011.

Ron DeSantis was elected governor of Florida in 2019.

In 2023, Sarah Huckabee Sanders became the first female governor of Arkansas.

Kathy Hochul became the governor of New York in 2021.

GOVERNING A STATE

The governor has an important job. He or she is in charge of running state business.

Who is the governor of your state? How do his or her decisions affect you?

GLOSSARY

appoint (uh-POINT): to choose someone for a job or position

budget (BUHJ-it): a plan for how much money will be earned and spent over a period of time

enforce (en-FORS): to make sure that a law or rule is being obeyed

executive (ig-ZEK-yuh-tiv): related to the part of a government that carries out laws

federal (FED-ur-uhl): having to do with the government of an entire country instead of a city or state government; the national government of the United States

legislative (lej-is-LAY-tive): related to the branch of government that makes and changes laws

National Guard (NASH-uh-nuhl gahrd): a volunteer military organization with units in each U.S. state

pardon (PAHR-duhn): to free from being punished for a crime; to forgive

term (turm): a definite or set period of time; many state governors are elected to terms that last four years

vetoes (VEE-tohz): refuses to sign a law that has been passed by a legislature; usually, vetoes can be overturned by a majority vote of the legislature

THINKING QUESTIONS

1. Which branch of state government includes the governor?
2. Where do most governors live?
3. How does the governor manage a state's money?
4. How does a governor work with a state's legislature?
5. Who is Sarah Huckabee Sanders?

INDEX

ABOUT THE AUTHOR

Francie Dolan is a writer from Seattle, Washington. She is an American history buff who loves to learn about how her country works and how it has changed over time. She jumps at the chance to travel to Washington, D.C., and visit the capital's important buildings and monuments.